Conversations with the stars

Heshanie Tennekoon

BookLeaf
Publishing

Presentation by *BookLeaf Publishing*

Web: www.bookleafpub.com

E-mail: info@bookleafpub.com

ISBN: 978-93-95784-29-0

First edition 2022

DEDICATION

Dedicated to dreamers, cultivators, activists,
artists & to all expressive beings.

Roots

The colour of your skin
Tells the stories
Of those before you
It sings the song
Of your ancestors

Don't let them question it

The curls of your hair
Forms a connection
To your heritage
It weaves the fabric
Of your identity

Don't let them shame it

You are a continuous story
With roots of yesterday

Don't let them erase it.

Dear World

Dear world
You tell me that I am beautiful
And I truly feel it
I start accepting it
And then you tell me
that I am too proud
You say "She thinks she is all that"

You tell me that I am intelligent
And that my words speak volumes
And I truly believe it
And I start accepting it
 Again
And then you tell me
I am too opinionated
You say "She is too loud"

You tell me once more
 That I have the power
The power to change the world
To make a real difference

And there I go again believing
And feeling it within
And then you tell me
I am too much of a dreamer
You say "She thinks she is a change-maker"

The moment I get a chance
To raise my voice
And be all that I am
 There you go again
Doubting my ability

But this time
I will not let you

This time I will believe
And I will keep believing
Until I am the hope & belief
That I am searching for in the world

Whole & Glorious

Taught to be perfect
From the day we were born

How to sit right
How to eat right
How to speak right
How to behave right
How to breath right

Society taught us
We are not our own!

It's our body
But we can't dress it the way we want to

It's our mouth
But we can't speak the words we want to

It's our brain
But we can't dream the way we want to

It's our life
But we can't live the way we want to

A woman
Is not your property
She is the monarch of her own
free will

A woman
Is an embracer of curiosity
She is the epitome of dreaming

A woman
Is just another human being

A woman
Is whole & glorious
For all that she is

Dear Women

Dear women
I often question
How resilient you are

You fight against a world
That felt like it was never made for you

You think love is everything
That it holds a special place, status and virtue in
everyone's heart

But often you get blinded
And forget yourself
Forget to stand by yourself
First and foremost

You follow the sweet words of someone
Falling for them, heart first

But dear women
Be careful
As they don't
Love as deeply as you

Devine & Beautiful

As I grow older
I have grown to be patient
I have grown to love gently
I have grown to love tenderly
I have grown to love myself

I have grown to love
The shape that makes me a woman
Showing the battles
I've fought
For me & our future generations

As I grow older
I have grown to love my body
The curves and the bumps
The scars and the marks

Patient as I see it change
As I evolve into my
Truest form

I have grown to be grateful
As I transform into something

Divine & beautiful

Love

Often speaking of love
We imagine 2 souls
We imagine the things
We do for one another
We Imagine the distances
We travel for one another
All the lovely things we would say
To see a smile

But is to love
Also not to love ourselves?
Why is it that we don't think of ourselves as our
first love?

Why do we not go the distance for ourselves
Why do we not utter those sweet, loving words
to ourselves

The person that
Walks every step with you
Follows you and smiles back when you smile in
the mirror

Is loving ourselves
harder than loving others ?
Is being kinder to ourselves
harder than being kind to others?
Is forgiving ourselves
harder than forgiving others?

Maybe.

Maybe we needed to start young
But maybe, It's enough to start today

To start being gentle with yourself
To start thinking of that little girl
you saw in the mirror
And be kinder to her
And teach her
That love starts firstly
With yourself

Strings

I gave you my heart
Not just in half
But as a whole

You promised
That you would take good care
And take my pain away

You promised
That you would gladly bare
And take all that it has to offer

But instead,
You poured
More & more

Doubt and pain
Tears & Fears

Until I am overflown
With nothing more to give

And now, here I am
Lying down in my bed
Thinking of how
You played my heart
Like the strings of your guitar

Amongst the dreamers

I am dreaming of a love
That consumes you
That inspires you
That admires you

I am dreaming of
A touch that sends
Shivers through your spine
A look that stares
Deeply into your eyes
And speaks to your soul
that is your shrine

As moments fade away
And as the sands of time
Slips through your fingers
You are holding on to a love
That consumes you

But at the end of the day
The dream of finding such a love
Will become just that

A dream
You don't want to wake up from
Because it drives you wild
Just to feel like that
It makes you feel alive

But maybe for a moment
I will hold on to this dream
Stay amongst the dreamers
Squeezing every drop I can get
Of a love
That is written
Only in the stars

Ignite

I play out our conversations
A 100 times in my head
And in each of those scenarios
Everything flows so perfectly

I say something to make you laugh
You kiss my forehead & cheeks
Hug me so tightly
It feels like we are a perfect fit
Two pieces of a puzzle
Made to match

But every time I open my mouth
And start speaking to you
We argue
My frustrations
& yours
Slip out

We test our patience
We say things we don't mean
We hang up the phone
And leave those moments
With neither of us winning
Both feeling like they lost
A piece of their heart

All because we forgot to really
See through each other
Hear one another
Forgetting to remember
That we are there for each other
And always in this together

But my love
Please remember
Whilst the sun & the moon
Don't always see eye to eye
She still needs him to light up her night
And my dear
Without you
My heart too
Will not ignite

Miles Apart

One home but two corners
Together but distant

One roof but two rooms
Together but closed off

One bed but two sides
Together but alone

One love but two hearts
Together But miles apart

Through You

When I see you
I see me

I see a longing to belong
To be heard and understood

Your eyes filled with the same
Questions, hopes and dreams

Your heart filled with the same
fear, pain and love

We are the same
And yet we are not

We are neither above
Nor beneath each other

When I see you
I see me
Through you

Colourblind

No matter what the colour of our hair is
It fades into grey
No matter what the colour of our skin is
It wrinkles in age

No matter what our heritage is
It leaves us behind
No matter what we try to conquer
We leave it behind

Maybe
We need to live
In a world that is colourblind
Maybe there is more beauty
In black & White

Where we are not defined
By our exterior
But our interior
Where we are not defined
By our actions
But our intentions

There will come a day
Where we won't judge a person
By their looks

And until then

I am dreaming of a world
That is colourblind

An Echo

They Say
We don't belong to ourselves
That we belong to the society

We hear what they have to say
We believe their Judgment
We let it consume our lives

We become
But not our own individual
But a little voice amongst the crowd
Trying to break free
Drowning with opinions
And predetermined notions of the world

A deeper sense
of loss is growing within
Loss of our sense of identity
Loss of our sense of self
Moulding into something
We don't believe in

Or maybe
We are just unaware
Unaware that we are drowning
Losing ourselves

Becoming an echo
of the people around you
Good or bad

But not just an echo of society
An echo, that is hoping to create a ripple effect
Strong enough to break free and finally belong
Only to ourselves

An old friend

Often when growing old
We find that silence
Is a gift

We grow up with
opinions and noises of others
And then one day
It all goes away

People move & become distant
And you are left alone
With silence
An old friend

An old friend
Who will remind you of who you once were
Before society taught you to become
Something you are not

An old friend
Who will teach you to love
Your own company

An old friend
Who will show you how to embrace
Your bitter, sweet journey

An old friend
Who will help you break out
From the doubts of the mind
From the limitations thrust upon you

We may not always see you
As a friend

But we know we need you

Silence, O My Friend!

Disconnected

I am scared of living in a world where
People are so disconnected from emotions
And the ones they love

Looking for love
Through the validation of likes & views
Looking for love
In the screens of our phones

I am scared that I will become them
Trying to fill this void of loneliness
I am scared that I will join them
And start disconnecting
From my emotions
From my connections
From the ones that are next to me

Trying to be seen online
I am scared, that I will lose time
Fighting this war of attention
I am scared, that I will loose connections

Connected

Sitting here in the rain
Watching it falling
Leaving little drops
Of water in surfaces
Adds a sense of calm

The grass sparking
As if there are
Drops of diamond on it

The sky is crying
With me
Like me it's Celebrating
Every Side of Mother Nature
Every side of Emotions
There's a sense of peace
Knowing that I am too
Part of Mother Nature
And today
We won't be bright And shining
We won't be colourful and joyous
We will cry
We will heal
For tomorrow
Until next time

Inner Child

We have been told for too long
To be practical, to think logical
To let go of our inner child

For too long
We have pushed our dreams aside
Getting the practical jobs, paying the bills
Living for the weekend, and not each day

For too long
We have neglected our true call
Avoiding our heart's desires

Well I say,
It's time to take the plunge
To dream big, to work hard
Focus on our creativity
And let it flourish

Because today,
I am deciding to hold on to my inner child

Fools In love

I want to run down the hills
Never to slow down
In the middle of spring
I want to fall & get back up
And do it all over again
As I fill my heart full
With dreams & adventure

I want to feels the rays
of the sun peeking through the trees
while I stick my head out the window
With my hair flowing through the winds
In the old car that you used to pick me up in

I want more moments
Of my head on your chest
counting the strands of your hair
While I steal a glimpse of your lips
Feeling every beat of your heart

I want to get lost in the rhythms
Of my favorite song
Dance like nobody's watching
Not a care in the world

I want to get lost in the sound
Of the waves, as my toes touch the sand
Watch the sea kiss the shore

I want to sing till my voice is disappeared
In the crowd with my friends
Or hiking to the top of cold mountains
Singing our lungs out

I want more tears
From uncontrollable laughter
I want more scars
From chasing sunsets & rainbows

I want to get lost in the world
And make memories
Like fools in Love
With living

Be

Be
In the moment
Let the train of thoughts stop

Watch as the sky changes colour
As the birds rush away to their nests
As the wind sweeps away the leafs
Let your eyes wonder

Empty your mind
As you watch the passing of a day
The silhouettes of the trees
disappearing into the night sky

Watch as you embrace
all that Mother Nature has to offer
Let your mind unfold
don't question it

Get lost in all your senses.
Feel the cold winds
Smell the fresh air
See the colors of the sky

Be a part of the poetry of nature
Listen to the song it's singing
Listen to every beat
Feel every note

Just be
One with the world

Slow Growth

Slow down my dear
You are only human

You have the power
to move mountains
But slow down my dear

You have the power
To create movements
But slow down my dear

You don't have to rush
As you get lost in the luscious
Fields of comparison

You don't have to push
As you tumble from the glorious
Peaks of self-doubt

Take the time to heal
More moments to feel
To get to know yourself
Before you move

Your time will come
To conquer
To define

But for now
slow down
My dear

Unwritten

To feel as deeply as I do
Is both a curse and
A blessing

Like the winds of a stormy sea
I feel rage for things unfair

Like the gleaming sunshine on a flower petal
I feel the hope to inspire

Like the rising of a phoenix from its ashes
I feel my power to remerge

Like the dreamy stars on an endless night sky
I fuel my dreams & desires

I am more than an emotion
I am more than a feeling
I am ever growing
I am a story
Unwritten

www.ingramcontent.com/pod-product-compliance
Lightning Source LLC
Chambersburg PA
CBHW061321140726

47998CB00006B/2494